SPRINGSONG

SPRINGSONG

POETRY OF RUDI HOLZAPFEL
1960-2006

WITH INTRODUCTIONS BY
ULLA AND MARJA HOLZAPFEL
AND TERRY CUNNINGHAM

MAUNSEL & COMPANY
DUBLIN

Library of Congress Cataloguing-in-Publication Data

Irish Research Series No. 63

Copyright 2012 Executors of Rudi Holzapfel Literary Trust

Academica Press, LLC
Box 60728
Cambridge Station
Palo Alto, CA. 94306

Website: www.academicapress.com
to order: 650-329-0685

ACKNOWLEDGMENTS

All our thanks and gratitude go to Brendan Kennelly, Terry Cunningham of Tipperariana Book Fair, Mona and Hermann Beisegel of Bonn, Linda Murray of Seattle, Maggie Eagan, his longstanding Tipperary friend, Dr Robert West of Maunsel Press, to Mike Kavanagh, Blackrock bookseller and, of course, Elgy Gillespie (who initiated the project).

— *Ulla and Marja Cybèle Holzapfel*

CONTENTS

TIPPERARIANA AND ALL THAT ...
By Terry Cunningham

It was the IRA ceasefire of 1994-96 that led up to my meeting with Rudi and to the holding of the first book fair in Fethard in February 1996.

I availed of the window of peace to travel North to visit my old college days friend Jamesy Vallely and family in Armagh city, especially my one and only godchild Joanna, during the glorious summer of 1995.

Jamesy was now in the second-hand and antiquarian book business at Craobh Rua Books, and he filled me in on his new career and how the whole system worked or didn't work, for that matter.

I immediately liked the Book Fair idea as a "suitable' fundraising event for the Fethard Historical Society back home in Tipperary. Jamesy gave me the Antiquarian & Second-hand Booksellers in Ireland 1995-96 list and told me to contact his book-dealing friend Rudi Hopzapfel in Tipperary town, and that he would surely help us.

Rudi's entry on that list read as follows: "Pennyfarthing Bookshop, Main Street, Tipperary. Shop. Irish Language and Catholic. Valuations free anywhere in Ireland.' I noted the "Irish Language and Catholic' bit, neither of which seemed a great marketing pitch to me even then!

So on my return I sought out Rudi in Tipperary town and found him in the old Pennyfarthing Arcade on Main Street, or "my suitably subterranean kiosk, my underground reading-quarters,' as he himself put it. I told him my story and of course he helped us.

The first Fethard Book Fair was held the following year on the second Sunday in February 1996 in the Fethard Ballroom, with Rudi taking centre stage, literally right under the piano player.

It was a big success and the piano player also went down a bomb. But Rudi wanted to do more so he began compiling a list of all the sought-after Tipperary books that had ever come to his notice. He called his compilation 'Tipperariana.'

On the cover it said "Tipperariana: Being Notes, Pointers & Current Market Prices of Tipperary Books for Scholar and Collector Compiled for The Fethard Historical Society by Rudi Holzapfel,' and was ready to launch at the second fair in February 1997.

We organizers then decided to call that second fair "The Tipperariana Book Fair.' The name remains, the book fair is still going strong and is truly a Tipperary institution at this stage.

Then in 2002 we nominated our first Tipperariana Book of the Year and thus Rudi's addition to the English language gets a further airing and meaning every year.

During all those years I would visit Rudi in his shops (he was inclined to move about) and his "last stand' was up a grand flight of stairs where he traded under the ambiguous title of "The Poor Sinner Bookshop.' Whether he meant that he was actually poor and also a sinner or whether he was just poor at sinning I never did figure out.

It was nice to visit Rudi in his shop. We would talk and we would talk, there were always things to talk about. We could talk about why people don't talk to one another on buses or trains anymore and then we could talk about people who talk too much and then we would just keep on talking.

So Rudi's talking stopped seven days before the Tipperariana Book Fair of 2005. But the reading goes on and the memories live on.

I'm very glad the IRA declared that ceasefire in 1994.

Terry Cunningham

Fethard

BIOGRAPHICAL NOTE

Rudi Holzapfel was born in Paris, France in 1938, the oldest of ten children. His father was an art expert and a Shakespeare scholar, his mother a dancer with the original Bluebell Girls.

After the war—Rudi had spent some time with relatives in England to learn English—he followed the family to California. He graduated from Santa Barbara Catholic High School. In 1956 he was sent to Dublin, Ireland to study at T.C.D., where he met and married fellow student Ulla Stroucken. They have two children, Francis and Marja.

At Trinity he did his M.Litt. on Irish Literary Magazines which were linked to the fight for Irish Independence.

In 1966 he started to work on his Ph.D. at Leeds University on the Irish poet James Clarence Mangan. Arts funds being cut under the new government, he had to start earning a living, first as a second-hand book dealer, later by teaching English Literature in German, all the while writing poetry and publishing privately.

In 1989 he decided to return to his beloved Ireland. He took up his work on his thesis about J.C. Mangan again, which later became part of the first complete compilation of that poet's work.

He kept on writing and publishing poetry, and dealing in second hand books at his Pennyfarthing, later Poor Sinner bookshop in Tipperary.

In 2002 he fell ill and on February 5th, 2005 he succumbed to cancer after a brave fight, surrounded by his family and friends in Bonn, Germany.

BACK TO THE BUSHES AND THE SPECKLED EGGS

Rudi used to say that he started writing poetry to impress some girl at Trinity, or beat a boasting student pal at some college poetry competition.

Looking a little beyond that flippant remark, it seems his interest in rhyme and rhythm was first awakened as an infant and toddler. Born in France in 1938, he was the eldest of ten children born to an art dealer, Rudolf Holzapfel, and Mona Trew from the Folies Bergères. His first language was French, mixed up with Russian, German, English and even a smidgeon of Japanese and Chinese being spoken around him by his parents' friends.

His mother, a pretty English-born chorus girl, used to sing Music Hall songs and nursery rhymes and self-invented nonsense to soothe and amuse him. At the outbreak of war when he was two, he was sent with his pregnant mother to an internment camp in Besançon (they had English passports). His memories of this time are enshrined in his poem "Winter 1940.'

His father was an antiques dealer with a great love of Shakespeare and the habit of reading aloud and reciting classical poetry. He had an American passport. Eventually, he managed to get Rudi and his mother out of the internment camp – but that was far from the end of their problems, as successive troops marched across France.

Later, Rudi was sent to London to learn English with his beloved Aunt Veronica before joining the rest of the family in California, where he went to Catholic Santa Barbara High School. Here, he met an assembly of very non-Wasp American kids: Irish, Italian, Middle Eastern Christians and immigrant Mexicans, and being a gregarious character he made a lot of friends and opened up to all sorts of different cultural experiences.

After his father's conversion to Catholicism in 1952—his mother had held the family together during tough times in wartime France and the turmoil after the war through her simple Catholic faith – Rudi found his first spiritual and global homeland in the Church.

By the time he was twelve he had encountered several languages and different cultures (and their respective mores and values)-possibly forming an amused distance from just one "national' world view.

His father sent him to Ireland "to get an education' in 1956. Here he found a people who had been disenfranchised for hundreds of years and had fought hard for their independence and faith.

His experience in America with the American poor and his respect for Native Americans had made him sensitive towards the plight of the underdog. "Pulling the pup from under the underdog" was one of his favourite themes in poetry and discussions. Becoming Irish meant that he committed himself to a people who had suffered, and to his first real "mother country,' one that was not a state or government.

Irish love for life and talking, singing and poetry (and love for their faith through times of suffering) spoke to his own easy-going nature, as much as lust for life and bravado (and Catholic piety) had also done when he encountered it among his Mexican pals back in the U.S.

In poetry, he experimented with free form, strong rhythms, and brilliant images (see "dog" and "spell"). Lorca was one of his rebel heroes; at Trinity College, Dublin, Spanish Literature was his second subject after English Literature.

His "'foreigner's ear' with its distance from the English language, his realization of its multitude of idioms and punning possibilities, all made for eager experimentation and often funny and ironic use of English, thematically coupled with a strong dislike for hidden agendas in politics and the media machinery. Later, his mistrust of the powers that cheated the underdog often turned into long rants against power groups in politics and public life. He always enjoyed a good fight over politics with friend and foe; but whatever the philosophical or political abyss that lay between them, he'd usually end it with "Oh, come on, let's have a cup of tea..."

Over time he turned towards more traditional verse forms to express love and pain in his personal life to illustrate human frailty and defeat, and the brutal subjection of nature by the materialistic values of modern age. The quest for romantic love and the fight against the "committee men" turned into an awareness and appreciation of all suffering, of mankind and creation in general (see "Steel and Glass' from "Sonnets').

The Sonnet form, long dear to him from Shakespeare, plus the acceptance of the inevitable loss of loved ones and of ideals: these eventually tempered the fury, outrage and desperation that so often exploded form in his earlier poems.

Still, in spite of all inward-turning and more structured poetic form there remains a joyful love of life and an ironic view of things. Deceivingly easy rhymes end with a surprising punch line bringing back glimpses of *Heine*.

Often you seem to be cantering nicely along on his lyrical horse, till it throws you off into a wheat field of laughter, wisdom and joy of life. The two last couplets of the Beachball in his last book "A Tiger Says His Prayers" speak of this joy:

Let's let this verse reverse what men may say,
Life's old deflated beachball's full of bounce,
Let's go out there and rouse it, make it rise,
And share with sun a moment in the skies.

Ulla Holzapfel
Bonn, September 2011.

FROM RUDI'S NOTES ABOUT HIS LIFE

Looking back at a string of books, broadsheets and pamphlets—many of them the frailest, fleetest, most idiosyncratic sort—I realize today what an exotic plant I must appear to some. Sheer creative enthusiasm has led me astray literally dozens of times, and I must admit I have gone with it gladly aware, perhaps, that it is as much of inspiration as one like myself deserves. Inspiration is the crown to which all talent aspires, but when one is unsure as I am, what my real talent is and where my real talent lies, enthusiasm is, as we say in Ireland, "your only man.'

When I first started to write everything I wrote was towards publication. A Catholic with an American accent and a German name I wouldn't have represented the usual Trinity student of those days who was usually a British ex-serviceman, a Northern or Southern Protestant, or an English public school boy. I wasn't a team sportsman; I was no great shakes as a student; but I did see one far off possibility for notoriety if not immortality and that was publication as a poet in one of our college magazines (I was eventually published in all three). My father had a large poetry brought back from America in 1957 and I reckoned the word 'poet' would be a good enough term with which to describe myself.

Armed with D.H. Lawrence's *Pansies* and Eliot's Waste Land I literally bombarded Icarus, our chief literary publication, until one day Ron Ewart, the editor, approached me saying "we know all the different poems in different colour inks and with different nom-de-guerres are by you but we have decided to publish one item we like.' From such base beginnings did my muse rise out of the depth—pure word-smithing, a barrage of pretensions, nothing else.

It didn't take long before dissatisfaction set in. At home my father's opinion was sought. It must have been six or seven poems later that he ventured to allow the word "talented' to pass his lips. But this for me was "damning with faint praise' as he knew English classical poetry intimately. Nevertheless I persisted experimenting with different meters for different effects and trying to marry modern idioms and classical prosody.

Formlessness was the name of the day. I rebelled and became formal. I had become great friends with Brendan Kennelly, a charismatic young Kerryman, and in our first book together we were determined to give rhyme and metre a fighting chance. This more formal aspect permeated all four of our books together ….

Taken from the unfinished notes excerpted in Marja Holzapfel's introduction to 'A Tiger Says His Prayers' – the last collection by Rudi Holzapfel, 2006

HE SANG THROUGH PLEASURE AND HE SANG THROUGH PAIN

When passing through Fethard I always think of my dad. These were his old hunting grounds. He simply had to be here once a year—even in the end, when he was already very ill and hardly in the shape to tackle his beloved stall at the heart of the occasion.

"Tipperariana" was a term Rudi coined. This is no coincidence as Tipperary stood for all he loved and had carefully chosen for himself. Cappaghwhite, his home Moanvaun, his neighbours and friends, the book stores at Cashel and Tipperary Town, all these made up the haven, the long hoped for refuge he had so long done without, working away as a teacher in Germany.

His book stores were in perfect order. All were welcome at any time and many took a book for free, because my dad would rather have seen a book with its rightful owner than with none at all. Even after his death people would come to his store and say, "He left this here for me—he wanted me to have it." Hour long discussions would ensue and cups of tea be drunk. Communication was the thing. In more ways than one.

My father wanted to write one last book to be called "Passion's Chapel"—it was to be on "the nature of love." This is a very central theme that flows through all his works: compassion and love. He never got around to writing the book, but the thought finds reflection in virtually all of his poetry, whether poignant and touching or ranting and raving. One day he said, "Isn't it funny how a face you first see begins to change after a while… you notice all kinds of things that didn't seem to have been there before." Extremely alert, he would notice the subtlest of changes until he had what he wanted: beauty.

The poems in this collection were selected by his family and friends. Having been given the opportunity to get something together for Rudi's beloved Fethard event, we quickly decided to give this project a purely personal touch. Those who knew my father well are perhaps best equipped to say which poems reflect the many, very different facets of his rich personality. Rudi maintained that "the man and the art are indivisible," and to this sentiment this collection attempts to do justice.

Future scholars will find in his poetry a vast "kingdom of the mind"—a sensitive, inquisitive and intelligent child's view of the world around. Rudi was rebellious in the way that he viewed things afresh, almost innocently and very independently. To peruse his vast poetic inheritance is a big task and not for the weak hearted. It is assuredly an endless one. He used to joke that his poetry would only be read after at least a hundred years had passed, if ever at all. He knew the full value of "a little known poet," as his lifelong work on James Clarence Mangan suggests.

To have a selection of poems picked by those who knew him intimately, however, is a real chance for anyone who wishes to know more about him. Here are those who knew and loved him and his complex personality, and can spot this in a poem. Here, we also have those who heard Rudi speak about his poetry and the poems he himself esteemed highly, such as "Dawn Clouds" and "The Star Chamber," "An Irish Mother Tends her Sick Child" and "When We Dead Awaken". Finally, "The Tumor" and "A Tiger Says his Prayers" serve as a cool diagnosis of his terrible cancer later in life.

Just before he went into hospital it was snowing outside. It was a cold and dismal February day. In his opinion the month of February could only be beaten for dreariness by November, which he considered even worse. "No this no that, no nothing: November" is what he used to say. Still, on this day in February, when the tumor had finally taken over, he leant out of the window, looked at the snow falling silently and said, "It's beautiful."

In years to come his poetry will speak for him—he knew that. The grandchildren he so longed for and never had the opportunity to see, Helen and Douglas (little Rudi Bear), will get to know their adventurous grandfather through his poetry. Here and now, his comrades and loved ones, his friends, his wife, his witnesses, his children—we are here to tell those who wish to know what he was like as a man.

Finally, I want to thank those who had a hand in this selection of Rudi's work. Aside from my mother and myself, Mona Beisegel, my father's sister, and her husband Hermann, and Maggie Egan were involved. A wife, daughter, sister and brother-in-law can certainly sing a song on the subject of my dad, but Maggie Egan was his poet pal in the final fifteen years or so. Maggie, herself a very fine poet, suggested a large number of poems in the book. A suggestion or two also came from Linda Murray in Seattle and Steward Hildred in England. We thank Terry Cunningham for his amusing and very astute input; it made us laugh! Elgy Gillespie from California got it all going and saw it through—no easy task—with Dr. Robert West of Academica Press.

The hardest thing, apart from deciding what goes in, was deciding what doesn't! Otherwise, we would probably have ended up with a Collected Works. Some poems not in this volume that would be of interest to an ardent scholar or any intelligent child are "Old Clothes", "Blasted Oak," "Not Just the Dark." Poetry, My Heart," "Here," "Figures in the Mist," "Loss and Gain," "I Understand," "The Nameless," "My Home," and many more. Feel free to look them up in Rudi's many other works.

A first Selection of Rudi's poetry called "Ask Silence Why" was published in 1987 and edited by the late Ellen-Shannon-Mangan. Ellen, herself a poet and a good friend of Rudi's also had a hand in my father's final work, "A Tiger Says His Prayers", published in 2007. As my father's poetry makes up a kind of poetic biography the next project will be a second *"Selected Poems "* to span his poetic inheritance covering another good twenty years. During this period he wrote some of his best work—*talent tempered by form*, as my mother put it.

Poetry was important to my father but it wasn't all that mattered: the glance, the action, the quick, compassionate gesture, the blessed intervention, the ready smile. The man, the feeling, the deed—these were inseparable from his poetry. I think in action he felt he had to live up to the high standard he had set for himself in his writing. But at the end of the day, in some lonely place in the small hours of the morning this must have dawned upon him:

"Poetry, my heart—the raw, the rhythmic beating:
Reality—when all the rest is fleeting."

Marja Cybèle Holzapfel
Bonn

The Beachball

A dawn of slanted sunlight, five past six,

And June 19th as well—if they cared —,

A cameo of life here in the sticks,

A blessed heaven long since disappeared.

Rain is the forecast for the whole day long,

Rain is the forecast after days of dull —

But here's the poet-rebel with his song,

His arm around a loving heart that's full.

What matter, darling, if it rains all day;

We've sun enough for two and that's what counts.

Let's let this verse reverse what men may say —

Life's old deflated beachball's full of bounce,

Let's go out there and rouse it, make it rise,

And share with sun a moment in the skies.

2004

dog

top dog god wot mutt pup
is worth the woof of omnidog
i let mine bark the nights and days away

he follows me from moon to sun
and everywhere my doggies gone
he's been doggoned by everyone

the spirals of his masters voice
have held on hand his head at heel
he needs no leash no sex appeal

no bitch can match him catch him scratch
hangdog at room temperature
all hot dog in a sandwich bun

when she's on heat my dog is cool
all foolish shedogs act his age
so old hes cold so cold hes tired

no civilservant slipper tears
nor sunday page carouselage
all revel under parrot cage

no postman bites no cats worth snarls
yet everyone must hid from him
his nails so click on coffin lids

i have a dog his name is ill
and when I die ill sell you him
or will i leave him in my will   *1960*

Ask Silence Why

Wherein a word is used,
Therein analogy;
Therefore no word abused
By me with you.

Wherein a word is heard.
Therein a picture seen;
What picture do you see
When I tell you

That I am speechless wont,
And by four words tell
More than I should have told
One such as you?

My mouth, my hands,
My eyes don't lie;
Let speak no thing,
Ask silence why . . .

1961

4

Springsong

This is my utter Spring,
My end and ultimate,
And this my sorrowing:
I haven't had you yet.

I haven't had you yet,
Because I want you still,
The stillness in your eyes,
The churning of the mill.

The burning on the hill,
The poppies ting-a-ling,
The low lawns to the lake,
The sky, and everything…

The sky and everything
Is what I offer you;
I haven't got them yet,
So you will have to do.

What will you have to do?
Well when it's done, I'll sing
Some very very song
Of utter utter Spring.

1961

spell

luv could be love
if only we spoiled it
correctly

or mispilled it wrongly
correctly
you get me

when i know it
i nowk it i wonk it i kwno it
i know it so well

hellsbells
when you know it
you now it

then no it
and
oh

how we feel it
whenever
we fell it

seems better

to spell it

somehow   *1961*

I Fly Before The Fury Of Her Love

I fly before the fury of her love!
No cloud caught out behind the wind,
Disastrously alone, has flown
With half so spurred a mind,
No petty thought a God,
No flower the battleside,
Nor light the stricken blind;

I fly before the fury of her love!

I am no bird that hastens home
Do not question as I come, for now
My flight, accelerating light,
Plows over the Plow, awheel, aspin
Detonates towards the dimmest sun,
An incandescent cometon
In the overseas of the galaxies,
Swimming for the shore behind the stars;
Ask me when I am gone,

It was the fury of her love I loved,
And all its anger pressed against my pride,
And all its loving buried there beside.

1963

My Love and I . . .

My love and I,
When we our vigils keep, agree
The most beautiful thing we have ever seen
Is our son asleep, and we

Almost impossibly together,
Cyclone and feather, stone and poetry,
Dream in him now the dear, the good,
The necessary other

And do become of all time's trinities
The steadiest triumvirate—of child,
Of girl become a mother
And animal at rest.

1963

In A Private Garden (for Mona)

    watching the windless willows weep
hangdown over the bloodgreen reeds
    water lapping to the edge of things
washing the wary moon
          is (!)
    Upsy Toady Willow Weep
caught in the whole of a hootowl's woe
    lolling lilypad lifting slow
sign of the seeping spring
        ahem . . .
    loveleah Toadeah Willow Weep
Todeah, don't you evah sleep
    deep in the bowels of the bloodgreen reeds
waiting for spring to come
        (burp)
    no'm Toady Willow Weep
no'm nearly fast asleep
    deep in the peep of a bulbul bird
waitin' fer spring t' cum
        ahum
    willful Toady Willow Weep
waiting till spring has sprong'
    (honey's hands like hunterhounds
hurtling out of the moo
        (oh oh)
    ooooooooooooooo

oooooooooooooo
        oooooooooooooo
oooooooooooooo)
                    n
        watching the wind up willows whip
swaying over her glutgreed need
        sorta slapping at the state of things
wiping the weeping moon
                    (sniff)
        who would not weep for Toadylas
shuddering silently once or twice
        mist like a mesh on the lilypond
the last line left alone

1962

Portrait

Ulla thinks I'm drawing her
Black on white as she draws me,
    I'm not, uh-huh, and here, you see,
I'm painting her and she, well she

Has hair, perhaps, like gold, maybe —
Wild red hair, so wondrously . . .
    Her legs are like, I like, you see,
So like her legs, so nice, and she,

She wears a coat shc bought in Bonn
Wristlets hidden (like a nun),
    A big fur collar and all that on,
On a bright green bench in yellow sun;

Blue skies, brown trees and orange hair,
Pale pink girls who stare and stare.
    (Small grey men who never dare)
She drawing me, I painting her;

On a sunny day in Stephen's Green,
First fine day in a fine first year,
    She drawing me, I painting her,
The whole world smiling hard and clear —

On a sunny day in Stephen's Green,
Blowing, blowing in the Spring,

Busting the inviolate Spring,
Violent, ultraviolet Spring!   *1962*

La Muerte (Death)

(In southern climes we make her a woman and look forward to the affair . . .)

She

Came quietly on a donkey
Or two, through a thin line of tree,
Sat herself down on the too wit grass,

Alass,

To woo: I'm done, my God, Ed,
Oh no, and other things she said,
A most marvelous pain in her ass:
They pass
Daway to her hell brown hair,
Blue, gree, now, rrrr, their white eyes were
Awhirr where blurred her deftly clever

Cleaver —

How she sing-sangue, coffin down
The bubbables of every drown
In that never, well, hardly ever

Sever . . .

Someone aaaaghed, threw in his gear;
Women came "round to hip and cheer
The death of men; had the wise but leapt

Not kept

Pieces of would through which they
Beheld her spectacles for free
They would have laughed, having slipped or slept,

Not wept

Me.

1965

Song

What we wanted was the Guts of God
(Our wish was His command)
God, He came with His Glorious Guts
Flowing from His Fine Right Hand

They were not green and gangrenous
Nor white and trembling thin
But bubbling, red, majestic Guts
Full of yards of Pain

Butchers burst from out our midst
And butchered Them up for us
Our rookie cooks "Eat up, eat up
We've made 'em taste real nice'

We gobbled all we wanted, so
The button popped the shirt
(Hors d'oeuvre of Appendix
Duodenum for dessert)

'Twas when the meal was over
And we tried to shit the bill
We knew we'd made a bloody hash
Of the best Bowels of them all.

1965

Leda and the Swan

"Did she put on his knowledge with his power. . .?"—W.B. Yeats

The big swan came with his hanging wings
And his big wings beat gigantic;
She asked him, "Sir, are you Jupiter?"
He answered, honking, sic.:

Honk.

When that was over, and over again,
They watched the naked boys
who swam to and fro in the dark canal
Dangerously near the noise:

Honk.

Said she, "If you ain't Jupiter, sir …
(And pouting she stretched a leg)
What will I tell me protestant pa
When I lay him a catholic egg …

Honk?'

"Thonk!' he (said)—Oh she was mad,
"You really are a beast."

Your feathers are leather and your beak is weak . . .
"You must be Zeus at least! (?)'
Nonk.

'Twas all he said and done,
And taking his leave of her
He flung two wing-fists full of the air,
Setting the eve awhirr . . .

Hoonnk!

That honk—It'd given her twice the know,
She was just another goose
As she cycled home on half the power,
Plain old fashioned loose.

                                        1965

The Old House

That house we stopped to see—but only walls

Remained … and ivy clung them thick and green:

Four hundred years ago its harp-strung halls

Had rung with brogue against the Ginger Queen;

Here Spanish sword-ends stirred the fires that shook

Each red heart's gloom, and there a child's laugh clove

The night to where the chained saint burned for book

And rebel rode the moon-lit maid of Love.

And now? The high hawks to their young are dead,

And noisy wheel around the ruined pile

Those carrion beaks who've made a nesting shed

Of Patrick's wild Ireland. "…and in a while,"

"They crow, "the walls themselves will fall, and sure . . .'

No carpenter, I work on roof and door.

1967

The Employee

Is all that fire put out, that passion spent

On bugger all, that I now worry what the boss

May think, and how to pay the bloody rent?

So I'm the rebel digit on his loss

Account . . . well, damn him and his cookie shop!

Can't I dream, and love, or try and treat all

Passers-by as human beings and drop

A bob from off some battered article?

I tell you, Mate, to please one poor old face,

To make it laugh again, or even smile,

I'd T.N.T. their bastard commonplace

And have them running up and down the aisle.

It is not time, but give my ghost-rebirth—

I'll burn away such sickness from the Earth!

1967

Poor Mangan

"On Friday, the 23rd he was buried in Glasnevin, only five people, according to
Brenan, (Father Meehan says three) following his remains to the grave … not a
single Dublin paper "marked" the funeral in any way, except The Irishman.
Mangan's small funeral, in a country like Ireland where "a good funeral' is one of
the consolations of the people, is almost inexplicable.'

(O'Donoghue's Life, pp 222-3).

The brave heart beat and burned till each bright vein
Ran riot with its scarlet love; that Genius too
Should crowd his noble head and that the man —
More spirit than a man—die then this dog's adieu . . .
O tragic paradox! But none there be
Who serve the Good God well and in material
Their rightful recompense receive. The fee
For Love and Loyalty, Faith, Goodness, Courage, all,
Seems one compendium of confounded pain.
And yet in him the Gaelic bards, outlawed and mocked,
Their language levelled, found a champion;
In this poor ghost, bewigged and ludicrously frocked,
Who from his land could glean no honour save
The five (or was it three?) who saw him to the grave.

1967

The Winter of My Words

When in the winter of my words she wanders,
Who was the summer once and sweet content,
Intending spring is down and gone forever
And autumn but the dead leaf and the wind.

Well would I take her from her little corner
("T' was chosen for its dear and friendly dark)
And show her, as a friend would, from a window,
The bitter hill beneath each boulevard,

And dry the lovely eyes that large with sorrow
Still yearn for lands we lost when we were young,
Before my dreams confused her every vision,
Before my lust tipped acid to her tongue.

But I am hard because the world is harder;
The times, with rope and whip, have called the play,
And lashed us through the hard, God-empty seasons,
First tightly to each other, then away . . .

So let me now in this, my severed era,
Sing her a simple song that one can keep,
When in the winter of my words she wanders,
Lest in the silence of my snow she sleep.

1974

The First Poet

The first poet
     Was the first ape to know pity,
And his first poem
     The tears when his dog knew pain,
And the first book
     The loss of love through lightning,
And the first reader
     The falling rain.

1974

Disappointment Diamond

I held you up into the light;
    You turned my eye the colour of the night
        And then you blew —
            Disappointment diamond you!

The sun took shape within your form
    And vivified your fire and ice;
        Why didn't you take his good advice
            And come on warm?

You couldn't start, I couldn't stop,
    And tho' I took you with a baby's trust
        Cold can burn; I let you drop;
            We bust.

Friends of mine console me now
    And say you were as cold as stone,
        A moon bejumping holy cow,
            And wonder how

I could have wasted all that time.
    I wonder, too, that I could feel
        For a little rock without its peel
            Sharp enough to cut through steel.

But I'd have shot this lyric lark
  And played blood-brother to a shark
    To have held you near when it grew dark,
      Disappointment diamond you . . .   *1974*

When We Dead Awaken

   When we dead awaken
After dark and dream have taken us
   One from the other,
     Shaken us
As the wind shakes out the carpet of the shore
And the sea breaks cold and white and pure,
    And nothing, no, not the thin bond
      Brother and sister share
    Be left us as we leave, O lover,
      Lover do not grieve!

     One day at dawn,
    The curtains of the water drawn,
Preparing for the golden-blooded sun
    To roll in on applause of sand,
      Hand will to hand
    Too softly for the worldly sound
      And eye to eye
    Need precious little of the sky —
   Doubt and dark and dream forsaken,
When we living who are dead awaken.

1974

Two At Night

    (I)

To have held your body close upon my own,

To have known the soul of you was moved by me,

I'd have scoured the crowded depths of hell

And searched an empty heaven for eternity —

And then (O miracle!) I held! I knew!

Who knows now nothing surely any more

Save what sad experience teach,

Save the wind above the long sea's roar . . .

    (II)

As the lover, after loving,

Lies without a murmur and is sad,

And in his wild, wild heart's confusion dreams again

Of having what he has had and had and had,

Compassless, companionless and cold

I float the wide, arterial sea

Between Reality and Dream,

Dream and Reality . . .

1974

Broken Bird

Broken bird,
Your wing's in place now;
You can hop around.

Don't do it so
Sadly, tho';
You hug the ground

Like some Cinderella's
Slipper
Still unfound.

I know
My window's
Not the great outdoors.

That my bleak inside
Is black
And filled with sores,

But it's winter there
Beyond my sill as well —
And cold as hell.

Forgive me my rough hands;
I found you sick,
I bound you with two rubber bands

And slipped a little
Wooden stick
Between;

I was the surgeon of your woe,
But I was clean
And had the know.

I should have tried
To do what poets do, perhaps,
And died.

I watch you now.
You limp, and stare . . .
I feel the fever in your brow

And tho' I never tear my hair
I lift myself so often
From this chair

To weep in silence, looking out,
It would do me
Good to shout.

I too am hot;
My habitat is not

This stuffy room
Filled full of history,
Mummified ideals
And gloom.

We'd both prefer the death
That waits for us outside,
But your small breath

Would freeze
In minutes flat —
No coat and hat,

And I would wander
Like a clown
Who's burned his tiny circus down.

Child of flight,
Your yearning has defeated me.
My eyes

Are full of your imprisoned skies.
I do not want to see
You suffer like some entity

Destiny has doomed to pain.

I try again.

I sing.

I talk to you of Spring.

But, O, I fear

You will not last the year:

Mend my heart,

Broken bird,

Something's missing, something blurred . . .

1974

Quiet in the City

Quiet in the city now,
Buses are in their shed;
The last whistler's stopped, even
Gamblers are in bed.

The stop-lights stare
In all directions, red or green;
A stray cat scurries
Over the road's rain-sheen.

A little breeze, a little dew,
A little coolness in the air,
A little place I know . . . not far . . .
Must get there . . .

. . . Get there before the sun comes up
And blinds my eyes,
And no dream dreamed
Between its setting and its rise.

Man needs a dream
To divide the awful day;
Man needs a bed to sleep in
And a girl to lay,

And booze that's cheap,

And a kid to treat,

And work you can come home from

Not too beat,

And a lot of courage,

And a little prayer

When the stray cats scurry

And the stop-lights stare . . .

1974

Old Cowboy Death

Call me, old cowboy Death, and I shall come
Easy as any woman when the lights are out:
Wailing caliope, crescendoing tympanum —
And all the sounding symbols poets clout
You with—nothing to do with it. The noon
Will not be reckoned high, nor the dark air
Blaze with showdowns in some midnight low saloon
As I walk in. Your dusk and dawn will share
My cactus sky to break and lay to rest
In unison and you will close your eyes,
And I shall say two words in final jest
And drink a little of your dark surprise:
Death, when you are ready, I shall come;
I shall be ready too, it will be time.

1974

To the Crashing of the Sea

Here upon the shore I wander
To the crashing of the sea;
The past gone and the future going,
What's to become of you and me?
Time's upon us, Angel, and the present
Weights us painfully,
The present, powerful as the ocean,
Powerful as the sea in motion,
Weighs us . . . painfully.

'Twas all of the sun and sea and sky
That sang the day we met;
The sun soared, infinitely high,
And I remember yet
That there were circles in the sky
Some call birds
Which should have warned us love would die

Despite cyclonic words.
And yet, like trailing tails of planes
That sheer across the blue,
The smoke of love has lingered on
Tho' the fire of love is through,
The smoke of love has lingered on
To cloud and misconstrue

My thought of you.

The same old sea and sand and sky

Turn to a sun that starts to sigh

Like a silver sea-bird, wings outspread,

Or a golden temple, burning red,

Or a Buddha's diamond eye;

But the sun, like love, must always bind

The will to bless with the power to blind.

Stare at it!

No, not the glare of it,

The sad, uninterrupted sigh of it

Is what we cannot learn to bear;

For us the seasons' brief revolve

Does all too coldly shape and solve

The problem of our distant share:

Me here, you there . . .

Seas and seasons separate us,

God and His graces seem to hate us,

Only darknesses will mate us,

Dogs adore our vivisection;

A year has flown and love is older,

Each little pebble here's a boulder,

And all the seething sea's asmoulder

With some evil predilection:

Your face grows faint
In recollection . . .

The ember of your hand
Cools upon my shoulder . . .

I grieve! I grieve!
Not for the cold, contented
Mishappenings of the human head,
For, from the moment of their wretched birth,
They are already dead;

But, for the hearts that young and heaving
Once ran the shining sand believing
And lie now stilled by dark begrieving,
My grief flies ever forth:

And I cannot put in words
Its thousand, thousand birds.

Darling, sad and thoughtasquander,
Here upon the shore I wander
To the crashing of the sea,
To the pounding of the ocean,
To the crashing of the sea,
To the pounding of the sounding ocean
Surging out to sea . . .

1975

Your Hands

Your hands,
Like sad ghosts
Dreaming out of sleeves,
Seem often,
Impalpably,
To float about me
Looking for ways
To soften
And caress.

My fists
Unfold like roses
When they near;

The callouses
All mutineer;
And when your fingers
Seek them
Even
Knuckles disappear

Sometimes,
Pale sisters
On a plane,
Yours are all
Folded, nervous,

Set to fly,

Some secret eye in them

Containing

Every move I make.

And when they

Cannot take it

Any longer,

And feel that they may

Burst

For passion and for

Pity,

And only mine

Can slake their thirst,

And only mine

Can bring

Clear waters

to their tiny city

With touches of a mild,

Mating kind,

Then,

With a blind

And willing love

Devoid of darker lusts

They come:

And, oh, how those

First, faint

Finger intertwining thrusts
Prove
The revo-
Resolution
Of their love!

And we touch palms
As on a Melanesian isle
Beneath a twilight sky . . .

1975

Now Is the Autumn Failing

Now is the autumn failing, leaf by leaf,

And the twilight fleeting from the rounded hill,

And the shadow growing on the ruined wall,

And the dark sky pressing to its final grief:

It is the dusk of day and year, and tho' the brief

Time beckon still and lovers smile and dream a full

Moon to the dark, wise men merely fear, pulling

Night upon themselves to find some wrecked relief

In sleep. And O' tis clear the Age is failing too,

Tho' its decline be drawn and imperceptible,

And only poets noticed in the spring that was

Something in the wind much crueler than the snow,

Something in the birded cherry spent and dull,

Something in the warm skies bland and treacherous . . .

1975

Anywhere Cafe

Remember the Anywhere Cafe?
It was down on Whatever Street,
When we were still in upward love
And our young knees would meet;

I took your hands at the table
"Jesus, I'm glad you've come . . ."
And the grey-suit brigade turned and stared
With a touch of opprobrium.

I held both your hands in my hands
And dreamed up the craziest things:
"We'll marry on Dhaulagiri, o.k.?
. . . with Buddhist wedding rings."

You touched me ever so gently,
And I cursed my precipitant words,
As you looked beyond, and the downgoing sun
Blackened a white flight of birds.

A look came over your features
More sad than the final mile,
Till you suddenly sighted and turned and gave
One radiant, delicate smile;

You weren't saying yet it was over;
You were hoping it might be done,
As you whispered "I love you . . . I love you . . ."
And I thought it had all begun.

I spilled half my tea as I did it;
I lifted your long white hand,
And kissed with a passion deep and dark
At the little gold wedding band;

I should have known at the time, tho',
Our death-knell had already rung,
But I looked and looked at that lovely face
With the songs I hadn't yet sung,

And I couldn't imagine me stopping
To love with the full of my heart;
I was so full of infinite goodness, girl,
I didn't think bad could start ...

Well, it's the same old Anywhere Cafe,
And I'm sitting here all on my own
With a pen in my mouth, composing,
And the grey suited swine are gone.

My friends recommend "The whorehouse . . .
Women are all the same . . ."
And when I say "No, she was different . . ."
They smile "Well then *you're* to blame . . ."

But no one's to blame here, surely,
Our love just couldn't go wrong;
It's the Anywhere Cafe that's at fault,
Playing the same old song.

You heard it and guessed my madness,
You wanted to help, so to say;
You left me to keep me, I FEEL it,
And you blew all the swine away.

Remember the Anywhere Cafe?
It was down on Whatever Street,
When we were still in upward love
And our young knees would meet.

1978

This Thing

It always takes dusk
And the sun going down,
A touch of the night
In a cheap room uptown,

And the traffic outside,
And a pain in my head,
And the knowledge I've lost
As I lie on the bed,

For this thing to start,
For the eyes to take hold,
For the moon to come up
Very thin, very cold,

For me to see clearly
And reach for the pen,
And write it all down,
And love you again . . .

1978

Another Man's Wife

Can be your own; protect her; deepen her honour;
Throw a quiet veil of mystery about her, warm and dark
As any starting night inspired with spikes of stars;
Her moveless evening leaves must not be easily seen,
Let them lick the ground as cool as light at dawn—
But do not bring her down; endeavour to enchant her
With a higher world, and tho' it mean great labour
Transporting where the trees no long grow and breath
Is out in freezing cloud on locked heights of lone peaks
Where no passes are. There is always the green vale
Hiding, and a small log tent between blue streams
Where the wood's been chopped already and two exhausted
Souls can fall into a corner with the door unlocked:
Bathe her back to beauty, trapper, in your bed of furs,
And show her slowly what love is. Escape and tears.

1978

I Would Take You With Me When I Go

. . . if you were worthy of it, and I mean born again
Of fury's fire and ice, ruffled by the red wind,
Driven vertically to cloud, steeped in some swampy fen,
Far from their cowardly calculus: your blue-eyed mind
Too dangerously high and fine for any man's mean fool
To deem Life's long emptiness fed with a brief shove, —
Wild enough to swim the hills and walk the black pools,
Your white flesh full of passions far surpassing love.

I'd not go traipsing back with one like all the rest,
Clever little seamstress subdued by a thick prick,
Ready to pass the gravy, tho' she'd failed the test;
The most beautiful woman in Greece would make me sick
In minutes over the darkest, most enchanted beer,
If she were a cow. If she didn't have it HERE . . .

1978

One Frail Rose Cloud

One frail rose cloud,
Sweet flower of the sky
Implanted, my Angel,
In the earth of my eye.

There to grow in soft passion
On the fields of the blue
Till it reaches such beauty
I pick it for you.

Keep it close to your heart;
It will help when you cry,
One frail rose cloud
In an evening sky . . .

1978

Within the Shirtsleeves

She lies within the shirtsleeves of the sun
A grief asleep, the warmness and the wind
Light in their caresses, for the Dark One's
Done her down and the Day Star to rescind
Has interposed with sleek and molten power
And laid himself beside her, full of cream,
To touch within the turning of an hour
That place I could not even reach in dream.

And I who'd kill to have her in my arms,
And I who'd die to plunder like the breeze
And snatch her up and swift her out of harm's
Way far beyond the further beaches' seas,
I know now what we lovers have to do:
Be priests, be poets, button up our pants;
Give God a chance to kiss where Devils grew,
And turn away, and like it, even dance . . .

1978

The Star Chamber

Lay down your lovely head and go to sleep
And do not mind the wailings of the world;
Tho' skies be dark for you, and all the deep
Confusional sea lie in your body curled
Yet shall I shield you from the awful night,
Postillion placed to guard one holy dream,
His eyes on things so deep and recondite
They are to other but a seem-to-seem:
You will not hear a sound above a thought,
But slumber swiftly through the starry park
Which lust, fierce tears and tender care have wrought.
And when you wake I'll have endured the gloom,
A little tired, that's all, your guardian ghost,
Still loath to leave the soul that loved him most.

1978

You Can Tell That They Are Lovers Still

You can tell that they are lovers still,
Their white hands cry it now they are alone;
Their eyes seek out the faint and fabled hill
The sun can never find when on his own.

And all the day their separation grows
And slips them into depths they never knew:
She starts to cry when someone cuts a rose,
He shuts himself indoors and says he's through.

And if, come dark, you chance upon their sleep
And stalk the shadows to each lonely room,
She lies as cold as death beyond his keep
And he's the stone upon her empty tomb.

But when at dawn the winter winds are drear
And little birds are losing to the sky,
There's something in that distance hot and near:
Just watch them at their windows eye to eye . . .

They're eye to eye tho' lands are tall between,
And heart to heart tho' months are flying past,
And mouth to mouth in kiss, and prayer, and spleen,
Still promising their love will last and last.

1978

The Cowboy's Prayer

Ah jes' upped n' swung et
Roun' by th' tail n' bashed
Et 'gainst muh ol' brass bed,
N' then jumped awl over
Th' goldurn thing wuth muh
Boots on 'till et were flat—
Ter n' a mean ol' Missoura
Pancake. Then ah rowled et
Up in a big bawl n' nailed
Et 'gainst muh den wall
Wuth a pole-axe n' three-
Inch screws n' shot at et
Frum a distance a' four feet
Wuth a slug-fed sawed-off
Fer sumthin' approachin' a
Week. Et were a glor-yus
Sight, son, wuth more holes
In et than a kosher gruyere.
    Hot diggedy dang ! ! !

1980

A Girl in Granada

(for Dodie)

The little girl with the wasting disease
And only two months to live
Walks with her mama down the street,
And a poet begins to give:

The eyes of the others who pass me by
Are dipped in the down of delight;
She walks with her mama, eyes on fire,
They are filled with the endless night.

Arms like sticks and legs like bones,
Black hair stripped of its shine,
All hope gone from that hollow face
And death in that crippled spine,

She taps at her fat mama's elbow
With a touch both vacant and vague,
Like a corpse stood up for a moment
In the charnel house of the Plague.

How can that woman show her about
On avenues teeming with life
To tall young men in light-weight suits
Looking around for a wife?

Love? Justice? Madness, perhaps?
Just doing the usual thing,
Making believe that a walk downtown's
The way to a wedding-ring?

Maybe it's simply to show the World
That the End is nigher than near,
And the death of a daughter's a damned good start
To the reign of the God of Fear.

The crowds, they glow and they glitter;
The people, they bustle and buy;
She passes so close I could touch her,
I touch her, I stop and I . . .

I've lost her . . . no wait . . . no, I've lost her,
No, wait . . . I've lost her . . . she's gone . . .
I've a great respect for a virgin death
(She fled like the falling sun)

"I was down from the Sierra Nevada;
My face was hairy and dark;
My hands were cut from the climbing;

"I was sleeping out in the park;
Like a gypsy in leather and silver,"
Like a parson, all pangs and remorse,
I'd have welcomes the wings of a woman
The way bandits welcome a horse.

It was there, the *paseo* at twilight;

The sky gone a paraffin blue:

Me chewing on half of an orange

And wanting a woman or two;

It was there, near the snows of the summer,

There on the prowl for a wife,

That I saw in the dark of the distance

Death with his arms round Life.

I've forgotten all of the others

Who look a man up and then down,

Their large cool eyes full of promise

As they search like cats uptown,

But the face of the girl with the wasting disease

Haunts me, pushing out hope;

This world's full of pain and disaster

And the young god of love is a dope.

1982

Where There Is Beauty

      (for my son, Francis)
There is beauty in the little grey
Houses side by side, and the ruined
Fields behind void of white flowers
Because of the thin, booted children.

There is beauty in that black building,
Tall, long-muscled and steely-nerved,
Windy-waisted ruiner of an environment,
Stationary rapist in the moonlight.

There is beauty in an old De Soto
Taxi chugging away in stopped traffic
While the full air of Athens chews
Away at the pillars of the Parthenon.

There is beauty in the squat square
Of a burned-out bunker reinforced by
Brown barbed wire, its twisted scanner
No longer reaching up in radar revenge.

There is beauty in the Cambodian mob
Putting the finishing touches to a
Woman tortured twelve hours for helping
A sick soldier across the street.

There is beauty in the long dead dog
With the fleas gone because the worms
Came and the worms themselves starting
To go now that the bones are showing.

There is beauty in the dead lake with
The soap-sud sides and the slow clouds
Heavy with soot reflected in its dark
Flat face fill the acid rain begin.

There is beauty in the brutal film,
Hero transfixed and screaming on the
Lance of his once-trusted friend now
Coldly watching the blood run towards him.

There is beauty in the laughter of the
Young mother whose baby was torn out
Of her and is now lying in a supermarket
Bag by a hospital waste-paper basket.

There is beauty in the sweat pouring
From that little blonde kid's wizened
Face as he screws his brain dry during
His absolute final chance at maths.

There is beauty in the gone dry place
Where the waterfall used to be, but now
The river's been turned around to feed
Turbines lighting suburbs all the same.

There is beauty in the after-battle dusk,
Men hanging heels first and heads purple
From trees split down the middle and
Blue-black from a napalm bombardment.

There is beauty in the derelict hearse
Picked clean, set on fire and then
Stoned by seven young Puerto Ricans
With nothing to laugh about but death.

There is beauty in the terror of a
Family huddled around the telephone for
The fourth call from a man they know
Has already murdered their smallest.

There is beauty in the young woman
Tying up loose ends and very carefully
Placing the bomb in the box she hopes
The postman will deliver promptly.

There is beauty in the groan of an old
Miner with dust on the lung listening
With his hand raised slightly and his
Eyes closed to a girl's medieval song.

There is beauty in a whole forest of
Trees with leaves too small because
They grow near Sao Paulo and Brazilians
Are always crazy before Lent begins.

There is beauty in the big spread ass
Of a sweaty jew businessman turning his
Glass quietly upside down at a blue film
To show the waitress that it's empty.

There is beauty in the tall young nun
Flattening her breasts at first light
And feeling the cancer bursting beneath
The little white cap of promised good.

There is beauty in the careful range of
An agent arguing with two old women who
Promised to buy an annuity but changed
Their minds and bought a sailboat instead.

There is beauty in the tired soldier with
A map of the world resting on his shins,
Suddenly realizing how small the faraway
Place was which cost him both his feet.

There is beauty in that magic moment at
A cocktail party when all of the people
Present are either lying, boasting or
Flirting and no honest soul remains.

There is beauty in the bent back head
Of an old Jehovah Witness beaten with a
A Bible and sitting in a room in Russia,
The blood trickling down from his eye.

There is beauty in the worn-out whore
Lurching back to her grey habitation,
Nose punched in by her gay pimp fella
And feeling the spread of the disease.

There is beauty in the old cat creeping
Along with its kidneys aflame while the
Man who loved it most shows a next-door
Neighbour how to repair a lawn-mower.

There is beauty in the young man just
Sewn up again, the sponge beneath him
Soaked in gore and his wife lying into
His clear blue eyes, promising him life.

There is beauty in the Japanese tenor
Singing his heart out at "La Scala",
On the last aria of his final night
Because one of the bosses is a queer.

There is beauty in the mad woman left
By herself at the top of the asylum,
And the flames climbing, and she getting
Into a full bath humming and waiting.

There is beauty in the boy holding the
Rat in the bottle of water, watching
It die; and every time the rat comes up
For a gasp he gives it another shake.

There is beauty in the once honest
Civil-servant committing his third crime
Because the state is corrupt, nobody
Tells the truth, and what of it anyway.

There is beauty in the mountain-climber
Looking back from a stretcher at the
Peak which he never climbed but which
Cost him a back broken and both hands.

There is beauty in the purchase for a
Great sum of a wonderful old bottle of
18th Century port, then opening it among
Friends and finding it undrinkable.

There is beauty in the young lady with
The nervous twitch trying to keep her
Face steady while talking to the man
She has loved secretly for six years.

There is beauty in the limping teacher
They all make fun of trying to win over
The worst child in the class while a
Sneer spreads slowly across its face.

There is beauty in the savage killer
Battering a thin dark woman who just
Won't die because all the heavy things
In the cottage have been hidden away.

There is beauty in the bald and ageing
Abstract artist quite aware the pendulum
Is swinging the other way and that soon
Nobody will want his yawning torsoes.

There is beauty in the bishop closing his
Accounts' books and realizing he's not
Much more than a crook and that Christ
Wouldn't want him if he died right now.

There is beauty in the teenage spastic
Trying to eat a piece of cake and drink
A glass of milk and dropping, spilling,
Cursing and pissing at the same time.

There is beauty in the scarred cougar
With a tear in its side and the snarling
Snub-nosed kids leaning on the pointed
Stick they've jammed between its ribs.

There is beauty in the forty-year-old
Housewife holding an X-ray up to the
Light and looking past death to the wild
Fields and flowers and hills beyond.

There is beauty in the rusted frame of
An old racing-bike stolen, stripped and
Left to rot still catching the sun and
Lighting the eyes of a drowning swimmer.

There is beauty in the hurt look of a
Badly-drawn nude in an oil-painting at
A country auction when there is laughter
Among the farmers for a certain reason.

There is beauty in the small boy staring
Up at a strange woman's house and seeing
His father briefly at the window, then the
Curtains being drawn, rain and silence.

There is beauty in the 404th placed Irish
Poet with his nose in a full glass kidding
Himself he'd be top banana in a better
World when he knows that's just not true.

This is where there is beauty, and tho'
There are other places I'm tired now and I
Can't think of bloody auld beauty anymore;
I must go to bed or I'll never get up in time.

1982

Like a Sapphire

There is more dark than light,
There is more distance than intimacy,
There is more void than matter,
There is more unknown than known;

Light, intimacy, matter and knowledge
Are as suns before the Sun
In the huge void of the Dark,
In the vast dark of the Void;

They brighten our world,
They embellish the earth,
They cancel out the dirt,
Make us sorry for our filth:

Only here on this earth
Are dark and light divided equally
Into day and night, joy and sorrow,
Knowledge and ignorance;

Only here on this earth
Are nearness and farness
So completely equal that they
Are both something and nothing;

Only here on this earth

Can intimacy abolish distance,

Is there matter enough to fill the void,

Is there as much known as unknown,

Yet only there on the moon

Can a man on the outposts of hell

Look back at the beautiful earth

And call it a sapphire.

Ptolemy was right

And Galileo wrong,

But you need to walk along the night

Before you can sing that sort of song.

1982

My Ecological Christmas Sonnet

The snow's a perfect . . . brown along the streets
Of new towns knocking on the wilderness,
Fitting image of the irremediable mess
They have made of all that's natural. Sheets
No dream could sleep on hang there cold and wet,
Their "whiter than white' grey-beige and yellow-
Pink against the one last patch of Christmas snow
Spiked bikes and big black boots have not yet
Crucified. And as the hammers bang, bang, bang
With Santa going, going, gone, The Schoolfed Kid
Has trapped the Snowflake God and shot him dead.
And all the wise have heavy heads that hang
Like necks with eyes upon the knotted snow,
Not caring to look up to rich, green woods . . .

                    . . . they too must go.

                                    1982

The Upturned Earth

Her shadow lies there on the upturned earth,
His shadow lies there on the upturned earth;
They're standing close, coats opened, knees inclined,
Embracing in the round arms of the wind.

He sees the distant hills, their rise and range,
She sees the far-off woods, and it is strange
How feeling grows beneath such open skies,
How feeling grows till they must close their eyes.

Her lips are cold; they carry such a thrill
That his cold lips whisp only of her will;
Like sweets that children can't afford, the taste
Of other tongues, the urge, the need, the haste . . .

Not quite as swift as birds are in their flight,
But faster much than couples of a night,
They make of this vast field in which they've fled
A very strange, a very upright bed.

And far away, and very small and straight,
A farmer sows his fields to sun that's late;
Erect against the wind he feels two blows, —
The upturned earth, it shudders and it knows.

1984

Dawn Clouds

I break my frozen windows to the cold
And let the chill wind spark me into sight;
The room runs on behind me, dank and old,
For I am flying in my mind. First light!

I see the clouds, the elephants of the dawn
Trunk-to-tail along the lowest sky,
Their slow sway-backs a flaming orange hue,
Their great, intrepid heads upheld on high.

What dust do they know out there at all?
They have broken the chains about their feet,
And are trampling down some vast apocalypse
Much vaster even than the one we'll meet.

Silver shafts control their golden eyes,
Their bluegrey hides are huge but deftly drawn;
They tread on marvelous valleys, full of flowers,
Up miles above our elemental spawn,

Heedless, in their mute magnificence,
Of the Devil's thin and drifting laughter,
Trumpeting their light between two darknesses:
The one of the Before, and the one After.

1975

To a Blackbird

(In memory of Francis Thompson, English poet, 1859-1907)

I hear thee calling from the eaves at night

When Spring's pale moon drifts very thin and cold,

And lovers haste like clouds through dreams of flight,

The young on wings of woe behind the old.

Impassioned darkling! From yon windy twig

Thy clear voice climbeth where the ethers leap;

Beyond the fragile flowers and fisty sprig

Thou heav'st thy heart out to a world asleep.

Ah me! "twere wiser far to drowse and dream

Than lie here left to mine own sullent thought,

Whose filth and doubt are but a turgid stream

Flung foully upwards our some Satan's grot.

Gold love thee, bird! From evil far estranged,

Thou canst soar upwards past these paling walls

And see the lovely dawn about these ranged

And pray they prayer in cloud cathedral halls.

Thou little mindless thing, thou flick of flaws!

Thou knowest nought of all Man's right and wrong,

And yet thou holdst God's Truth in tiny claws

And singst for thou hast got the Gift of Song!

Thou art mine own brief miracle outdrawn

As I towards the Coming Brightness glance,

And know it is a dark thing brought the dawn,
And know my darkness, too, must stand a chance.   *1987*

Frances Farmer—Not Forgotten

You started fierce – and fought your way across
Parents, teachers, peers and the police;
A lively girl in love with freedom, tossed
In an asylum, screaming for release.

And who can say how much you suffered there
Every degradation, every vice;
The tangles gathering in your lovely hair
And nothing left you tender, fresh, or nice?
A willful, wanton woman in a trap,
Too straight for Satan's hometown, Hollywood'
They dragged you down, then laughed and stood you up
"Hey, whatcha doin',—tryin' to be *good?*'

Misled, misused, misunderstood, still thinking
There had to be a way, you found the answer,
Got your act together, stopped the drinking,
Then had to fight the thing that killed you: cancer.

I'll not force you further, nor coerce my rhyme,
For, revels all, we three abhor the rotten;
I stretch my hands across the Field of Time: -
Francis Farmer, you are not forgotten!

1991

The Moving Tree

     (for my daughter, Marja)
That tree up ahead
  Has come to a stop;
    Look! even the leaves
      Too tired to drop;

A tree stood straight
  In a twilight sly,
    Like myself at times,
      Grown half too high;

Doomed to go lonely,
  Always at odds,
    Food for forked lightning,
      Fighting the gods …

Hey, tree … you know what?
  No need to be sad,
    We've got each other;
      Things ain't so bad:

As I come towards,
  Put my arms around,
    Love ya and learn
      To stand my ground;

Will you, my friend,

   Will you learn from me

      How to be kind of a

      Different tree,

So some future guy,

   Whatever his groove

      Learns from a verse

      How a tree can move?

1991

Iraq

Come, let us praise our heroes of the air
Who fell their fiery loads with such precision,
Obedient to that chieftain of the Chair,
The Great White Father, King of Cold Decision!

A claque for them, bold warriors of the clouds!
Brave navigators, pilots, bombardiers…
Who rain their death on kids and huddled crowds
And then scoot home to drinks and rousing cheers.

Be lavish in your lauds for these fine men,
Americans and British, fighting French, -
What better way to get the auld boot in?
Beats hand-to-and on hill and gaping trench!

Applaud, applaud…till everlasting fame
For the courage of their distant blazing ways
Surrounds them with the
   STINK OF SIN AND SHAME
For the thirty thousand killed (first seven days).

1991

Hooded Crow

Nothing can add a sweetness to his song,

His voice at best a chuckle at the dawn;

No one can put a rightness to his wrong —

He's Doom, by all accounts, superbly drawn.

And yet I welcome him as morning lights

To leave this scavenger upon my sill

As if exhausted from those Summer nights

That for the gloomy mind bode mainly ill.

And as I slip to where he struts and stands,

The window raised—the glass without a drink —

I reach to lift him in, yes, *loving* hands ...

He scoots, of course, skedaddles, and I think

Here's Death, the very near, afraid again

Of that poor fool who wields the poet's pen.

1997

April Strange

Spring's loveliness is strangely cold
As in the breeze
Snow – pink, white and gold -
Falls from the trees.

Tho' sunlight floods the park
My mad mind soars
Through flowerstorms in the dark
To those snowflakes in the skies
They call the stars.

1993

May

"Tis May, and in the nest
Each tiny heart's awake.
Each bud, each living thing
From songbird to the snake.

As happy cries of youth
Reach up into the blue
A woman with a rose
Looks out upon the view.

A tapestry of flowers
Fills mountain valleys high
Like love that floods the song
Of water, earth and sky.

1993

We Rose in Love

We rose in love, like flowers that climb the sky
We rose. Before those ancient walls, that Ireland
So cherished by us both, we thought to try
Ad rise above the passion that is fire
To reach the Garden of the Kind and Good
That all-surrounds the comely House of God…
My Heart,—I fear we hardly trod the wood
Which borders on that broad demesne, nor did
Much more than view it from some sad afar;
Here, where the slaughtered fossils fail to scream.
Our love was neither flame nor even flower,
But the life-blood flowing from a dying dream.
And yet withal we spoke as poets speak:
Where other fell we rose, and were unique.

1993

If I Saw my Love with Another

If I saw my love with another I would smile;

All to myself I would think her in better hands;

I would know her happier down the winding mile,

From the cold cut of mountain to the tidal sands.

If I saw my love with another I would smile.

If I saw my love with another I would smile:

"Twould not be her mistake but mine, I'll have you know;

I did not fall in love to fall for just a while,

Nor did I fall in love to fail and die, as is the style;

I fell in love forever so that God could grow.

If I saw my love with another I would smile,

And I would dream perhaps she loved me somehow still.

Love has no logic; 'tis Wisdom's wildest child

I could see them heart to heart, bound to Passion's will,

And I tell you now, as I stand here, I would smile.

If never she returned, and if perchance she found

Another yet to take, for better or for worse,

Still would I believe in her, and feel the bright ground

She trod on full of flowers, and neither fret, not curse,

Nor weep, now even make the lightest, slightest sound:-

If I saw my love with another I would smile.

If I saw my love with another I would smile.

Only an owl, my friend, knows the worth of an owl.
I would smile if I saw my love with another,
Deem him the better man and call him brother, *brother*.

1993

An Irish Mother Tends Her Sick Child

All night I wake and keep vigil for you

That fever go and you may sleep, and through

The burning hours I watch and pray the beads

While you are turning fitfully, and needs

Beyond my ken are yours, and only prayer,

My lamb, to guide me through from here to there.

Last night the doctor came and washed his hands

"Tis touch and go," he said, "this thing demands

That we do nothing," and I searched his eyes

As he explained how viruses like lies

Will have their wicked way with love and youth;

How science wanders past the simple truth…

"It's like we lived two thousand years ago:

Call if there's any change." How old and slow

His movement through the room, that mighty man

Who could not help, himself so tired and wan

And wracked with doubts more troublesome than pain

Before he bent and washed his hands again.

Now all the night like some small bird at dawn

That goes from branch to branch when Winter's drawn

Its icy coat above the empty earth,

I go from prayer to prayer, the pain of birth

A little thing to what I'm suffering now.

How can I help if no one else can, how?

And what is it you want that I can bring?

A little song? Ah God, I couldn't sing

With you there worsening, babby, by the hour,

Too sick to cry and in some devil's power

That wants to tear you now away from me

And add one lasting grief to agony.

All I can do I do … my aching head

That longs to rest for seconds on the bed

Is full of words that surely Christ will hear,

And old St. Joe, to whom the child was dear

Is speaking now to Mary, nice and slow,

And she will intercede for us, I know.

And still I wake and vigil keep for you

That fever go and you may sleep, and through

The burning hours I watch and pray the beads

While you still moan from time to time and needs

Beyond my ken are yours, and only prayer

To guide us through, my lamb, to where …

                    to where …

1993

Like Keats

I feel like Keats. That feathers stopped outside

Sings beautifully. I mustn't have much time

As I fly once again above the wide

Dawn world, still stuck here with the same old rhyme

Pedestrian in this poor verse well short

Of genius while that loopy blackguard sings,

Showing his high heels. Should I just abort

When lagging there behind that pair of wings

For flying lower and for singing worse?

When is to continue the coward's way out?

Not often, thanks the Christ, but what a curse

When one's own song's no better than a shout!

Tho' second-best forever's where I'm stood

I feel his courage flowing through my blood.

2001

And Then the Sun

For one whole day high winds and threat of rain,
A menaced light, a moody, brooding sky, —
The clouds three different speeds and, strange with pain
The leaning trees all watching something die …
What weather this? What weather coming next?
No certainties, all whether, shore to shore;
Autumnal madness in a May that's vexed,
A Spring coiled up within a tightening core.
Then, in the distance, there's a dip of wings,
A kestrel in this kingdom of the crows,
A voice sky high that calls for better things,
As if in answer to a week of woes,
And then the sun sweeps in, more blessed than words,
With rhododendron blazing and the song of birds.

2001

Steel and Glass

I loathe cold Mammon's temples and can pass

The tallest best with crushing downward thought; —

In every doom-filled room a bleak Black Mass

Is being said, as all the stolen bought

On epic scale is mercilessly sold …

And yet, as plane flies up and sun descends,

I view with almost tenderness the bold,

Broad scheme of Man's travails to make amends,

Tack loveliness on ugliness and try

To find some way for some small part of art

Before his high-rise world is downed to die.

I too spew dust and hurt as I depart,

But celebrate the use of glass and steel: —

Strength tempered by Reflection's commonweal.

Toronto, 1998

I Laughed

I lived. I laughed. But as I did I sinned.

I loved—as Kavanagh sang—"not as I should'.

As I began I lasted till the end,

A rebel razzing every modern good,

A literate anachronism in

An age unworthy of the name of Man.

I was a knight, I cherished what had been;

For what was up ahead I said "I can.'

I held within my arms what had been killed

And thought to give it life with words divine,

But could not wake the verses that I willed

And ended up a-squeal with all the swine.

To weep, tho', were to die. I had the grace

To laugh until the tears ran down my face.

2003

Kingdom of the Stones

How can one love this Kingdom of the Stones

Where flaccid wolfhounds sleep in ruined halls,

And rain and wind and lightly buried bones

Raise conversations quaint as cannonballs?

Where stench of damp and sweat and turf and yeast

Assails the nose of lord who comes to laze,

And man with stick guides straying beeve and beast,

And there's great import in a turn of phrase?

A poet's land – Falcarragh down to Ring -

Where wooly warrior ken the price of peace,

And stop their wars to sport, to love, to sing,

To pray their devils do not find release, -

And every now and then clouds few and low

Breeze in with sun and warmth where roses blow.

2003

The Tumour

Who set the seed? Who started with the sowing?

Or was it simply preordained in time?

And all the while the bloody thing was growing —

Whose fault was it? Whose carelessness? Whose crime?

Who caused it, all the cursing and the crying,

For what in ages hence may seem a con?

And all the while the body knew "I'm dying,'

And all the while the mind just carried on -

And what the soul did in this era tempty,

The soul that ever wades through right and wrong?

The soul arrived at last at what was empty;

Contrived to keep on smiling with a song.

And as for that within which grew and grew?

It needed but the vacuum spirit knew.

2003

Building Sites, Dublin

Grey skies, and wind, and the gaunt shapes of cranes

Towering over the wastelands men have made

With their machines, while Man, crablike, complains

Over a fleshless carcass . . . We've put paid

To contentment with all our tugging greed.

We've robbed our souls and spirits of the Light

Till all is lust and appetite and need

And Summer's sun is moonless Winter night

We made our God convenient, then we left

Him glowing in our churches all alone.

Were we of Him or He of us bereft?

And now the hundred thousands mew and moan

That those who gave a hand now get the boot

Their wasted lives spent helping those who loot.

2003

Feeding the Crows

I look up slowly as I close the gate.

Some thirty crows are settling in the trees.

They flutter and they fret. They've learned to wait.

I stop a moment, stare, and as the breeze

Brings others wheeling in from out the skies

I think I know why they are gathering here,

The old insistence in their raucous cries,

That old ambivalence 'tween greed and fear.

How like ourselves they are, these souls of jet,

As they flock feasting on what's left and dead,

Suspicious still, no single one a pet,

Destruction always in that sleek black head.

I've strewn my scraps upon a stoney shelf;—

In feeding them I find I feel myself.

2003

September

September! Old Planet Earth has rolled right
Round again, and the winds are rushing leaves
Along the ground as the long-legged light
Plays tough and go with what is old and grieves.
Poor bard – in this sad world of hide and seek
If you're the best equipped God help the rest!
Your songs sing on, your shouts remain, you speak
Of Spring in Fall, your strange blooms stand the test
Of time and are scarcely less beautiful
Than all this sunlight stained with tragedy.
Soul and spirit, mind and heart feel the pull
Of a dusk that leans almost endlessly,
And all the while the cup of sadness fills,
The sun's a heavy head on pillowed hills.

2003

The Girl

Beside a leafless tress, a frozen lake,
Already now the girl has stood for hours,
To Life's last desolation wide-awake
Within the thrall of Winter's darker powers.
She stands there very silent, very still,
The tenements like cliffsides ranged behind,
Afraid to move, to speak, to voice her will,
No comfort and no warmth of any kind.
And some, at window, shake their heads and stare,
What brought her here? What brought her? What indeed!
Hope brought her here with every sort of care,
And left her coldly with a single need.
I ask you, how much longer must she stand
Before Love comes along to take her hand?

2003

Winter, 1940

Child in her arms, another in her womb,

My mother boards the bus for Besançon.

Amidst the tears, the all-pervasive gloom,

She smiles and waves goodbye as Dad looks on.

He told me laughing in his later years,

"She was glad to be rid of me, I think,

On her odd vacation to that place of fears,

Where soup and snow were all the good and drink."

Enthusiasm and simplicity

Were hallmarks always on her lovely soul; —

I carry them about as well, but me,

I'm often winter Midnight at the Pole.

A lovely nun gives up her window-seat

To keep me quiet as I enjoy a treat.

2003

A Tiger Says His Prayers

Head down, eyes closed, within the circus cage,

A tiger, paws together, says his prayers,

Releases for a time a rippling rage

And lays before his God his simple cares.

Enough to eat, enough to drink, a mate

Are quite enough if you are quiet of mind,

But Freedom's children only celebrate

When they have left behind their bars in bits behind.

To alternating flash of Death and Fear

The black and yellow shudder at his flanks:—

Shut up within this noisome jungle here

How sad to hear him growl his holy thanks.

His prayer is done. Again the monkey-screams.

Bring on the dark, dear Lord, bring on the dreams.

2003

At Dawn

I heard the blackbird sobbing as he sang,

Perched high upon his pinnacle of song, —

What lady listening to his dark harangue

Would not go dizzy with Love's come-along?

He sang through pleasure and he sang through pain

As if they mattered, darling, not at all.

Each time he stopped I hungered once again; —

The sorrow was quite lovely in his call.

Then back I thought to faces sad and fair,

Back, back to slender bodies, slender legs,

Back to the long dark, long blonde, long red hair,

Back to the bushes and the speckled eggs.

And then I saw the dawn, sincere and stark,

Rise up, and smile from what I thought was dark.

2001

INDEX OF FIRST LINES

BIBLIOGRAPHY

Cast a Cold Eye
Rudi Holzapfel and Brendan Kennelly
Dublin; Dolmen Press; 1959, 39 pp

Romances
"By rooan hurkey"
Dublin; privately printed by Dolmen Press; 1960, 30 pp

The Rain, the Moon (with introduction by Donald Carroll)
Rudi Holzapfel and Brendan Kennelly
Dublin; Dolmen Press; 1961, 62 pp

The Dark About Our Loves
Rudi Holzapfel and Brendan Kennelly
John Augustine and Company; 1962, 31 pp

Poems: Green Townlands
Rudi Holzapfel and Brendan Kennelly
Leeds: The University Bibliographical Press; 1963, 15 pp

Transubstantiations
Rudi Holzapfel
Privately printed; Dublin; 1963, 7 pp

Nollaig
Rudi Holzappel (sic) and Oliver Snoddy
Privately printed; 1964, 7 pp

Why Hitler is in Heaven (satirical ballad)
Rudi Holzapfel
Privately printed; 1964, 8 pp

Translations from the English
Rudi Holzapfel
Dublin; Museum Bookshop; 1965, 50 pp

Dublin Magazine: An Index of Contributors
Dublin Biographical Series I
Rudi Holzapfel
Dublin; Museum Bookshop; 1966, 118 pp

For Love of Ireland
Rudi Holzapfel
Broadsheet of nine poems; Leeds, 1967

The Rebel Bloom
Rudi Holzapfel
Privately printed; Leeds, 1967, 50 pp

Mangan"s Poetry in Dublin University Magazine: A bibliography
R.P. Holzapfel
Hermathena Nr. CV; 1967, pp 40-54

James Clarence Mangan: A Check List of Printed and other Sources
R. P. Holzapfel; Dublin, Scepter Publishers, 1969, 88 pp

Parasites Lost
Rudi Patrick Holzapfel and John Joseph Conleth Farrell
Privately printed; Cork, 1970, 12 pp

Rudi Holzapfel: A Bibliographical Check List
Alraune Graefin Boesewicht, 1971, 16 pp

Soledades
Bad Godesberg; The Sunburst Press, 1974, 83pp

Icarus 70th Issue, The Big Bed (excerpt)
Dublin; 1976, 13 pp

Whom a Dream Hath Possessed
Sunburst Press; Blackrock, Dublin, 1975, 111 pp

A Smile Dies
Sunburst Press; Blackrock, Dublin, 1978, 77 pp

Repeat After Me: Poems
With Hermann Brunken
Euskirchen; Woodway Press 1980, 57 pp

The Mask of the Red Life
Omdourman; Sunburst Press; Blackrock, Dublin, 1981, 24 pp

Poems Written Swiftly
Sunburst Press; Blackrock, Dublin, 1982, 107 pp

Buckshot (Aphorisms)
Sunburst Press; Blackrock, Dublin,1983, 55 pp

Turning and Manipulation. Miscellaneous Poems and Satires
Sunburst Press; Blackrock, Dublin,1984, 128 pp

The Light of Loss
Sunburst Press; Blackrock, Dublin,1987, 62 pp

And Other Poems
New York; Pioneer Printing, 1987, 41 pp

Ask Silence Why; Selected Poems (1961-1982)
Edited by Ellen Shannon Mangan
Dublin; Beaver Row Press; 1987, 196 pp

White Alligators; Poems and Satires
Sunburst Press; Blackrock, Dublin, 1991, 97 pp

For Ronnie (single leaf to be read at graveside); 1993

An Cheapach
Sunburst Press; Blackrock, Dublin, 1993, 68 pp

Collected Works of James Clarence Mangan: Poems 1818-1837
Jacques Chuto, Rudolf Patrick Holzapfel, Peter MacMahon, Padraig O Snodaigh,
Ellen Shannon Mangan, Peter Van De Kamp
Irish Academic Press; Dublin, 1996, xvii and 420 pp

Tipperariana:
Notes, Pointers, Current Market Prices of Tipperary Books for Scholars and
Collectors
Compiled for Fethard Historical Society; 1997, 37 pp

Dark Harvest; Poems and Satires
Sunburst Press; Blackrock, Dublin, 1997, xv and 75 pp

Sonnets
Sunburst Press; Blackrock, Dublin, 2001, 157 pp

Selected Poems of James Clarence Mangan
With Ellen Shannon Mangan
Dublin, Irish Academic Press; 2003, xx and 404 pp

The Thieves of Dream
Sunburst Press; Blackrock, Dublin, 2003, 55 pp

A Tiger Says His Prayers
Sunburst Press; Blackrock, Dublin, 2007, 73 pp